way-marks

way-marks

new poems *by* rusty c. moe

Fourth Lloyd Productions
Burgess, VA

For permission to repoduce selections of this book
please contact:
FOURTH LLOYD PRODUCTIONS
512 Old Glebe Point Road
Burgess, VA 22432
e-mail: stodart@kaballero.com

Also by Rusty C. Moe
Our Presence Together In Chaos, Black Moss Press
Where God Learns, Black Moss Press
www.books.rustymoe.com

Printed in the USA by Lightning Source Inc.
ISBN: 978-0-9717806-2-0 Paperback
Library of Congress Control Number: 2007926678

Book and cover design by Richard Stodart

Cover photograph, *Sentinels*, by Herb Hoover

For my family, my taproot:
Harold Allen Moe (1927-2003)
Helen Dorothy Moe (1929-2003)
Mickey Moe
and
Penny McRoberts

The trace that I leave will disappear from view,
but is not lost—it becomes part of the place.

—Andy Goldsworthy

I have my friends eternally.
We left our tracks in the sound.

—Neil Young

contents

angel fire

...dismiss what insults your own soul...
—Walt Whitman

Solitude—
where I begin to die
(where the mind, fatigued
by thoughts
of fate and knowing,
and the eyes, weary
of not being used
to see,
can slowly slow
and come to rest,
no longer smitten
with deciphering
the world),
hear me!

Solitude—
where God begins to die
(where harmony and history,
beatitudes and burnt offerings,
symbols and sanctuaries
dissolve
beneath the perfect surgery
of silence),
I have lost
what most needs to live.

Hear me
as I pray
to my own ambition,
as I chant
the ten thousand names
of my heroic self,
as I take
and eat
the mirror reflecting
my own
beloved face,
as incense rises
from the outflashing
of my own myth.

Solitude—
begin your pentecost
in me:
I am anxious and lost
in a fabulous land
bereft of miracles;
I worship
at altars finely wrought
by the terrorism
of desire.
I have listened long
to others
(tried to make matter
what matters to most,
dressed myself in titles
that promised prestige)
and trusted their voices

of blood and custom,
and yet:

I divine no sin
where sin should lay,
conceive no reason
for saviors or savants,
read scripture written only
by quills of cinnamon.
I need a new death,
a final death,
that returns me
to what I once was—
lit with laughter,
amazed by animals,
lacking all sense
of seasons and feasts.

Solitude,
servant of fire
(I am created
to wait
and be
at ease
within a core
of quiet joy)—
hear me!
Circle me 'round
with your burning wings
until I am
hidden
and complete.

a hymn from sixteen

...there in the cool dusk, with the waters of the river around him and the great pine giants whispering to one another, the area known as Sixteen seemed to Bert Church to be an Eden of its own, and so came into official existence the town of Edenville, Michigan.

—Stanley Berriman

I am so small
to be living
within
so much—
winter's fugue
resolving into spring,
spring ceding
to summer,
summer rearing
toward autumn,
autumn cradled
in winter's sober lap—
and the cycle spooling
around itself again.
Tell me:
what do I dare
by believing it?

I live among animals
whose names
do not matter,

speak words
whose meanings vanish
in the face of the animals'
windless trust.
My sins are absolved
by a host
of sparrows
eating scattered crumbs
beneath the window ledge.
The loon's wail
at eventide
exposes
the primal grace.

Who am I
in the compass
of history?
My battles
are inward,
my holocausts
unknown;
I liberate only
a few shaggy poems.
Revolutions come slowly
and leave few ruins.
Every manifesto I compose
dissolves
in the destiny
of each moment.

The inmost seasons
have no symmetry

and few discernible segues;
ambiguity their chiefest yield,
confusion their usual spice.
So I turn again
toward the atoning clay,
which offers me
snowfall and rainfall,
windsweep and wheatsheaf,
fruitsap and leafscreen,
fireshine and riverswell.
In those large and fearful hands,
I have no purpose
nor truth to proclaim,
no pedigree worth repeating:
my daring surrender
is Eden's declaration
that I,
vessel and vapor,
am her human hymn.

when my mother was dying, we ate ice cream

We won't recognize each other the next time we meet,
but I hope we love as well as we do right now.
—Stephen Levine

When my mother was dying, we ate ice cream—
moose tracks, vanilla, and neapolitan;
banana splits, root beer floats, Boston coolers—
ate from bowls
we'd used as children,
with silverware gotten free
with an order of pots and pans
bought from a door-to-door salesman
in 1960.

Clock-time was worthless.
Real time was measured
in breaths, hers,
and
by bead
after bead
of water
dropped
between her suckling lips
to cool the sting of gall
that seared her throat
after she vomited.
One daybreak,

I was singing The Lord's Prayer
to her,
looking into her slack and dozing face;
at *Give us this day, our daily bread...*,
she raised her weak arms high, high,
and, eyes still closed,
conducted an invisible orchestra,
and sang along with me
in her rosary soprano,
all the way through to the *Ahh...*
of the long *Amen*,
before dropping suddenly
back to sleep.

On Wednesday evening,
July 2nd,
the coin we called *Mother*
was spent,
and all the ones she'd merrily minted—
children,
grandchildren,
great-grandchildren—
witnessed
her Great Emptying.

After the *quietus*,
after everyone had left
but me,
the room was silent,
but not as silent as she.
I got on the bed

beside her
and pushed my face,
again and again,
against her hushed heart,
and swaddled myself in her smell
and sang to her again:
Softly and tenderly, Jesus is calling,
Calling, O children, come home.

I asked her:
Where are you?
Are you anywhere?
Was she in the land
of the Golden Harvest,
where saints are combined in love?
When Thomas Merton
was asked if there was
such a thing as heaven,
he said:
I don't know,
but if there is,
there won't be much
of you there.
Was Merton right?
Wrong?
Wierd?
Where is your new where,
my mother,
O, my mother?

Then we washed her.

My sister washed her hair and breasts;
I washed her face and neck.
My sister washed her belly and back;
I washed her shy cleft, my first nest.
We each bathed a leg and a foot.
We dressed her in a new nightgown
and remade the bed—
black, red, and white striped sheets—
folding the top sheet down,
just above her waist
and placing her hands
in an X
across the sheet.

Early the next day,
I followed the hearse
to an industrial park
in Bay City,
to the crematorium.
I helped two men wheel her—
now in a white-lidded
cardboard box
with *Helen Moe, Head*
printed at one end of it
in thick, black ink—
to a small room with a cork floor,
a dusty, plastic palm tree
in one corner,
and stainless steel doors
in the middle
of a warped paneled wall

in front of us.
One of the men—*I'm Jim*—
punched a button.
The doors slid open.
Fireclouds plumed
in the distance.
We raised the cart level
with the furnace
and pushed my mother
toward the clouds.
The doors slid closed.
Jim said,
When that blue light goes on,
the burning begins.
My eyes flicked
from the light to the doors,
from the doors to the light,
five or six times
before it blinked on,
very blue and very bright.
Jim turned to me,
I lost my mother two years ago. I'm sorry.
Ordinarily, you could wait,
but with tomorrow being July 4th,
today's one busy day.
I shook his hand and thanked him
and walked out
into the hot, vague morning.

in eden was the christ-child born

...for like a Edom's bowers
This plain doth sweetly hum
With myriads of bright angels
Who bid you welcome, come.
—Anonymous

In Eden was the Christ-child born,
by Adam was he named.
'Twas Eve who bathed the tiny light
while Mary rested, worn.

All 'round the plain did Joseph walk,
his seamless robes unfurled,
exulting, weeping, praising, thrilled,
tending this gypsy flock.

Beasts fresh-formed from silt and soil
moaned low and gathered near,
and Certain Ones with angel names
began their first noel.

By Judas was the moistened wheat
mixed, kneaded, turned, and baked
to celebrate the holy kiss
of Love bent us-ward, freed.

In Eden was the Christ-child born,
a dusty deity,
who, naked from first breath 'til now,
bids paradise return.

a poem for my father whom i never knew

I want to write a poem
about my father,
but I don't remember him.
I don't remember him
because I didn't know him,
even though I was 53
when he died
of a beaten-up heart.

His life seemed simple—
television,
Pabst Blue Ribbon,
deer hunting,
Mennen deodorant.
He met my mother
when he was 17 and she was 15;
they married two years later;
two years later, I was born;
two years after me, my brother was born;
three years after him, our sister was born,
and our family was set.
We moved 25 times
between my birth
and my high school graduation;
my father and mother
moved nine times after that.
Their last home
was in the done-over basement

of my sister's house,
a dim and pleasant place
that smelled of old tobacco smoke
and well-rehearsed memories.

My father had a near-death experience
ten years before his real death—
a palette of colors shimmering
within a voice
of pure light
that questioned him—
did he want
to stay with Love
or return
to the rougher loves
of body and family?
The instant my father said
Return
his heart was re-awakened
by electric paddles
in the emergency room.
I asked him
if he was sorry
he came back:
Yes—
I thought I had something else
to do,
but I never found out
what it was.

He only had one story
about him and me.

It was January.
You were six weeks old.
I was driving
your ma and me and you
to Albright Shores
in icy rain.
Just as we turned
onto Estey Road,
the engine stalled
and wouldn't roll over again.
I wrapped you
in a towel,
shoved you down
inside my shirt,
and we walked
three miles
in that storm
to your grandfolks' place.
I just knew
you were dead-drowned,
We were all scared to look.
I opened up my shirtfront.
The towel was dry,
and when I pulled it away,
there you were,
curled against my heart
like a wood shaving.
You looked up at me
and shot me a grin
I'll never forget.

When I was in my forties,
he suddenly apologized
for the many beatings,
many years past.
We were standing
on the dock
in front of the Beaverton house.
I asked him why:
Your mother made me do it.
When I got home
from work,
I dreaded coming
through that kitchen door,
knowing she'd be right there
starting in
before I even got
my boots off,
railing on and on
about how evil
you and your brother were.
The only thing
that would calm her
was for me to take
my belt to you.

I asked him what made him stop:
One Tuesday night,
pork chops were frying,
potatoes were boiling
for supper.
We were in the back bedroom.

Your brother had already
pulled his pants down,
and he was lying
across the edge of the bed.
I hated that sight—
those little white shorts
over his little butt,
him beginning
to whimper
and squirm
and squint,
and I hadn't even touched him.
She was there, too,
pounding on my back
with her fists,
yelling at me
to hit him—
hard!
hard!—
that he needed
to be hurt hard
for what-all wickedness
he'd been up to,
and—I don't know—
something in me snapped,
and I wheeled around
and lashed her face
a few times
with the belt,
and that shut her up.
Finally.

She ran out of the room,
ran out to the woodshed
and stayed there
the night through.
I pulled your brother's pants up,
and laid down on the bed
with him,
and rolled him over
into my arms,
and we cried together.
We cried.
That was the last time
I raised a hand
to either of you.

I wasn't with him
when he died—
the only member
of the family
who wasn't.
The moment I heard
the words
Passed on
he was near me,
then sweeping slowly
through me,
like a long-held sigh,
and I knew
he was happy.
I shot a grin

at his bare soul,
and he was gone.

Maybe my father
will tell me
about himself
in this poem I'm writing
because I didn't know him.
And when he speaks,
maybe he will remember
his True Name
and why he returned.

assist me to proclaim

O, Life, how long you are!
—Padre Pio of Pietrelcina

What is oldest
means most—
places, faces,
certain smells
smelled and named
for the first time
(lilacs, sumac, goldenrod).

They have shaped me—
for what I love,
I worship,
and what I worship
has whittled me
toward the truth
I carry (and long for).

Older now,
I am heavier
with the weight
of flesh
and memories;
losses no longer lighten,
delights descend to desire.

The constant call
of kin and comrade

swells the inner tide—
gravid, supernal.
No day,
no moment,
is ordinary.

The mystery shaped
by innocence
has been re-forged
in the heat
of sentience.
Wonders come sudden,
raw, and small.
Ancestors arrive
in dreams,
murmuring
of mercy
and its irrelevance
next to a life
lived gratefully.

I am weary
of holding
so much
for so long.
Release your servant
in peace.

eulogia

I am trying to learn yellow. It refuses me.
—Vincent van Gogh

At Glenstal Abbey,
I walk a path
to the icon chapel
with Auriol de Smidt
of Findhorn Bay.
I want to learn prayer:
it refuses me.
(Logic is foreign
to spirit:
maybe prayer razes
the fixed and formed,
leaving only liberation
in its wake.)

Primeval oaks and rhododendrons
surround the chapel,
which has been scooped
from the clay
inside the abbey crypt.
To step into it
is to step
into the region
between thought and dream,
between the eye and its color,
between the yeast and the rising.
The floor is fresco,

the walls
are of faces and flesh—
or so the textures
and the icons
have me suddenly imagining.
Outside the steel gates,
we hear skylarks
(their song reminds me of rain)
and the raspy-sweet
tswi! tswi! tswit!
of a nesting swallow.

Auriol motions me
to her side,
whispers,
The Madonna and Child—
see their tin clothing
and the way they peek out
from behind that tin frame?—
that is the way the soul
peeks out
from behind
our calcifications.
(Maybe prayer
is the soul's dream
of itself
after the
personality's cage
was locked
and the key swallowed
by society.)

I wander among the eyes
of men-made-saints
who mean nothing
to me—
Basil and Gregory,
Dimitri and Stephen,
Nicholas and Athanasius.
No gilded legend deserves
my robotic reverence.
And then the spell shifts:
and these flat faces
are replaced
with those I have touched
and kissed—
with Tim's
and my parents',
with my brother's
and my sister's—
faces defined
by ordinary sorrow
and unspent joy,
eyes riddled
with need and mercy.
Among this obscure remnant
that limps toward love,
I glimpse heaven:
Ahhh....
(Maybe prayer begins
when words fall
over the edge
of themselves
into silence.)

sto lat

> She...appeared to me as defenseless poverty—
> no relatives, no country.
> —*Raissa Maritain*

My mother's wedding dress
was rented.
Immediately after the recessional,
my father's father changed
into clean work clothes.
Pictures of that late, May day
show my mother's father
in a blowsy suit
that sexily droops
over his squatish frame,
a half-gone bottle of vodka
in one hand,
a dead cigar
in the other.
Everyone else
wears a flower.

My parents' *poprawiny*
lasted three days and nights.
The day after,
my mother kicked my father,
said she hated him
and wanted a divorce.
When my father
told me this and that

he wished he had granted
her her wish,
I was relieved through-and-through,
knew then why I felt
that I never belonged
to them,
had often yearned
for them to part.

When my mother was 13,
her mother, Pearl, died
of sugar sickness.
Before the coffin lid
was closed
and Pearl left her house
for good,
my mother unwound
the rosary
from Pearl's hands
and pocketed it.
She kept the rosary
until she died;
then we placed it
in the urn
with her ashes.

When my mother died,
only two brothers
of her 17 brothers and sisters
still lived.
Neither came
to her homemade funeral,

nor did they call
with succor—
kinblood had thinned
to the quality
of a glance
at a stranger's shoes.
We buried her
beside my father's family plot,
between his grave
and a bald cypress.

raḥamim

*...the idea that the millennium had already begun
freed them [the Shakers] from tradition and authority...*
— *John M. Anderson*

From the ends
of the earth,
bring forth My precious sons
(who have seen through death)
and My cherished daughters
(who hear the heart).
Each of you is My
anointed one.

Be not afraid:
I have gloriously formed you
(you are weighted with glory).
Listen:
I am calling you
by the name
you have been desiring
since before your birth.
From everlasting to everlasting,
you are My beloved,
and I am yours.

Be not afraid:
I am doing a new thing.
You will pass
through waters

of chaos,
and they shall not swamp you;
you will walk
through fires
of tyranny and fear,
and their flames
shall baptize and refine you.

Be not afraid:
I am wholly faithful.
Within Me, no one
is forgotten;
everyone belongs.
Before—
and after—
anything was,
I Am,
and I am with you.

Always.

know your bone

(for Robert Lax, 1915–2000

> *Know your own bone;*
> *gnaw it, bury it, unearth it, and gnaw it still.*
> *—Henry David Thoreau*

September, 2000
I heard
that the revelator
was coming home—
back to the United States,
to Olean,
where he was born.

I sent flowers,
celebrating your nearness.
Your niece called,
told me
you wanted me
to know
you were
in your bedroom
smelling them
Right now!
You died the next day.

November, 2003
Looking
for your house

on Patmos,
we climb spiral streets,
ask *Where?*
follow fingers pointing
Over there!—
toward cliffs,
toward the quay,
toward the sky.

Lax. American. Where?
I say to a man
carrying an olivewood staff.
Lax? he asks.
I nod.
Dead now. A great man!
he says
in a voice more joy
than voice
and points
Over there!—
toward the hills.

Finally,
here it is
(no doubt),
fifteen minutes by foot
from the harbor.
I laugh at myself,
at my idea
of a holy place—
a couple of

periwinkle blue propane tanks
sit on a fern-green stairstep,
a young cat basks
on the porch's half-wall
(I touch an ear,
and she stretches and writhes
in sudden rapture),
dingy bath towels
dangling from a stubby rope.

Thank you:
from this present-day cave
came your faithful letters.
Simple, unsealed revelations—
Hot, hot here—if ever
you plan a visit, don't make it
July or August. (October,
more like it).

Hidden manna—
Won't try a comment
on any big themes.
(Hear so many from visitors
in this room, just can't.)
Bruce Cockburn (hadn't heard
of him) comes on fine
for me.

Eating of the tree of life—
Lots of visitors coming by,
lots of unanswered mail,
& lots of very nice cats to feed

on (pretty small) front porch.
My thousands of cats
send your ducks an hello.
They have (no joke)
a limping hen
who feeds with them,
& has for a couple of years.

Rejoicing in the blessed dead—
One fine spring day
at the New Yorker office,
I heard James Thurber
& Joseph Mitchell
barking at each other
from open windows
across a narrow courtway.

Songs of marvelous angels—
I think Tom Merton liked being
the son of two artists
& being an artist himself.
(I feel he felt
he was part of a tribe
& knew where
he belonged in it.)
Some of our gang
(not I but others),
felt like changelings,
couldn't imagine how
they had been born
to parents
so unlike themselves

(not Merton).
My memory
of our whole life
as a gang is like the memory
of a jam session.
We were so much involved
in our present activities,
in the harmony,
we'd (blessedly) established
in them
& in the appreciation
of each other's
spontaneous contributions to it,
that we had little time
for childhood reminiscences
or family stories,
unless they turned out
to be funny.

You always signed
your letters
(to me and others)
with a yellow dot
after your name.
Someone asked you
what it meant:
Nothing at all.
Thank you:
we weren't born
to be anyone
in particular,

to accomplish anything
in particular;
we were born
to know our own bones—
to trust what it is
that supports us
and allows us
to bear our solitary portion
of grace.

fountain stone

I pray for stronger wings to lift the earth with me.
—Trappist Monk, "Brother X," 1935

You are among us
and within us,
always and now,
hallowing our homeland
with Your only Word—
our gifts and our deeds.
Thank You
for the grace
of our daily bread;
continue to open
our constantly-closing hearts.
Help us
not to be led
too far
from our true work,
for we want to help
build up
this good place
while we're here—
build it up in mercy
and gratitude
all the days
of our lives,
until we are empty.

O, Fountain Stone
from which we are cut,
let this be.

marks of a wayfarer

> *God breathes through us so completely,*
> *so gently, we hardly feel it.*
> **—John Coltrane**

—For what do you seek?
—That the burden of seeking be lifted from me.

I'm going to start
a new religion:
no hymns, creed, or saints.
no priests, pews, committees,
no bishops, buildings, missionaries,
and only one commandment:
proceed from a heart
soaked in yearning.
I'm going to start
a new religion:
don't tell anyone.

When I am gone,
what single breath
of mine
will be breathed in
by someone,
drawing him nearer
to the blazing dream?

Whose breath
have I breathed in today
that lights me up
and dreams me closer
to the faithful city?

I will name things
and release them
from the bondage
of being unknown,
and once they are known,
I will listen
to them,
and they will tell me
what they really are.

Love does not
call itself
love,
does not know
the word—
it sings instead,
and
you
me
family
earth

appear and disappear
within its music.

Prayer is not words,
ideas,
moments of feeling holy—
prayer is the moaning
of all
that is unanswered
and unfinished
in us;
prayer is the ache
of the unbreathed breath.

the time is at hand

What breathes through the napping cat
and the falling rain,
the cricket's song
and the mourning dove's,
the moving air
and the geranium's red?
What breathes through these things,
and all other things—
known, unknown, and unknowable—
connecting them in fierce designs
that call forth our grateful yearning?
I ask, *What?*
knowing all the while
that I am too slothful
to ponder such a question
for too long.
Mystery is not my *forte*:
I am made of too much dust.

taken by the secrets

1

Into your hands I surrender my spirit.
You took me from my mother's bowels:
my time is in your hands;
you are my wellspring.
From my youth,
I have been possessed by hope,
a wonder wandering among wonders,
endlessly, festively, proclaiming you.

'Midst my great sleep, I heard Your invitation:
Beloved, seek My face.

And my slowly-wakening soul replied:
I will seek Your pith and Your presence
my whole life long,
and with my whole life,
I will revel in Your covenant.
You are my cloak and marrow,
the primal vigor in whom I trust.
Your face shines, and I am saved—
and Your face shines all the more.
For one thing only do I yearn—
to dwell in Your earth household
with each full breath of my brief days.
Your law is unbegun love, honeycombing the soul.

You are the measure of all things,
curing and confounding the mind.
Your abundance is cunning,
reminding us of our littleness.
Your light sunclads the inward eye.
Fear of You is a merciful fire
that tenderly cleanses forever.
Blessed be You Who ladens us with benefits.

2

My throat reeks like an open tomb,
my attitudes grow fat and foul and make hell,
and you know full well my blasphemies.
My shame is hot within me,
and its tears are my daily bread.
Deliver me, my heart's True Code!
Make no tarrying
to gather my tears into Your weeping.
My soul longs for you
as a desert she-beast wants for new water.
Let beauty—like the silver, floating moon—
illumine me and show me
the work that I must do.
In your mercy, release my voice.
In my groanings, perfect your strength,
and deliver me, not unto my attachments,
but to the rock that is higher than I—
the body of Your glory.

3

Love the Lord, all you exiles!
May your soul make her boast in Him.

Your flesh is as stubble
before a wind that passes through
and never returns.
So while you are here,
touch and hear and taste and see
that the Holy One is wild and sweet,
and those whom He loves
(which is everyone)
are returned to their rightful owner.
Behold, the eye of the Lord is upon those
who watch for His bright blessing
as well as upon those who are unseeing.

Rejoice in the Lord,
and your face shall be cleansed.
Declare and desire the work of God
(there is no want in those who desire Him);
clothe your praise
in rivers glorious with melody.
God is our wealthy place,
our corn of seven colors,
our golden guide,
even into death:
open to Him in all times.
Strip your heart before Him.
He is our aged King, bearing fruit
even in the midst of our bleak shadows
and shallow dreams.

4

Those who have been taken by the secret parts
abide in that dark brilliance

where grace is ravished by the nard of truth
and chaos is kissed by the plump lips of peace.
There, they hear the Lord:
Beloved:
I am your hungering and your food.
I am your thirsting and your water.
I am your Eden and your Armageddon
I am your persecution and your protection.
I am your fellow-traveler and your destination.
I am your seeking and the sought-for.
Every particle of this winged world declares
that paradise incarnates.
In my left hand
is fullness of joy;
at my right hand
are pleasure-groves and pomegranates forevermore.
I am the name of your mystery.
I am yours,
and you are mine, O flesh,
O lovely clay.
Rest: in hope.

And my soul replies:
Amen, Beloved. Selah.

jesus wasn't jesus

> *...all darkness proclaims my Word—*
> *listen in the darkness, and you will hear it.*
> **—William Goyen**

Jesus wasn't Jesus
to the ones
who knew him first—
Alphaeus' sons,
Zebedee's sons,
Cephas, Andrew,
and the others.

Jesus wasn't Jesus
when he renamed people—
Rock,
Beloved,
Guileless,
Daughter,
or spoke his riddles—
God is like...
Love is like...
Faith is like...
Heaven is like...
or healed our dreams
of sorrow—
Arise!
You are whole!
You are forgiven!
Come forth!

or reorganized nature
with single syllables—
Peace!
Be!
Still!

Jesus wasn't Jesus
until he was unrecognizable—
a gardener,
a ghost,
a shadow frying fish
at dusk.

Jesus wasn't Jesus
until he was gone on,
and the ones
who knew him first
had to gather
without him
to re-create his shape
and presence
out of memory,
fear,
and cobbled hope.

friend of my final moment

...revelation remind[s] us continually of our role in creating
life, creating love, creating freedom, creating justice.
We can change from consumers to celebrants,
passing out the bread and wine to all who come to the table.
—M. C. Richards

The Trappists are not visionaries;
they do not seek conversions.
They practice the fifth gospel—
love lived, not preached.
They give their Muslim neighbors
a portion of their monastery
to use for daily prayer;
they teach them French,
deliver their babies,
tend to their health.
The monks consider
their presence
an affirmation
of the right
to be different
in a culture
that decrees
docility.

Christmas Eve, 1993:
Our Lady of Atlas Monastery
is invaded
by Muslim rebels.

Djamel Zitouni,
tells Father Christian de Cherge
that the monks must leave the area.
Father Christian says they will not.
Zitouni says,
You have no choice.
De Cherge replies,
Oh, but we do.
Over the next few years,
the monks refuse
to bend
to the demands
of the rebels,
refuse protection
of the Algerian military.

March 26, 1996:
midday Mass
is celebrated.
The gospel of the day
is from Saint John,
Chapter 8:
I am going away,
and you will seek me....
Later that night,
20 militants
from Osama bin Ladin's
Al-Qaeda network
burst into the monastery,
round up the monks,
lead them through the village
toward Médéa.

May 30, 1996:
three of the monks' heads
are found hanging
from a tree
near an abandoned gas station;
the other four
have been tossed
onto the grass nearby.
Muslim villagers
dig seven graves
in the small cemetery
beside the monastery.
The skulls
of Luc,
Bruno,
Celestin,
Michel,
Paul,
Christophe,
and Christian,
rest in long coffins.
Their bodies are never discovered.
Our Lady of Atlas remains empty.

Luc Dochier, physician, 82:
We can only exist as monks
by willingly becoming
the image of Love,
as manifested in Christ,
who, though innocent,

chose
to suffer the fate
of the unjust.
As Edith Piaf sang,
Je ne regrette rien:
No, nothing—
but nothing—
no, I regret nothing.

Bruno Lemarchand, priest, 66:
Here I am
before You,
my Beloved—
rich in poverty
and indescribable weakness.
Here I am
before You,
Who are nothing
but Love and Mercy.
I am here before You
whole and entire,
with all my soul
and with all my will.

Celestin Ringeard, choirmaster, 63:
In carrying out
my daily duties,
I sing
two little sentences:
O, God,
You are the hope

on every face
of the living,
and
Wonder of Your grace—
You entrust
to human beings
Your secrets!

Michel Fleury, cook, 52:
If something happens to us,
we want to experience it here,
in solidarity
with all the unknown,
innocent
men and women
who have already paid
with their lives.
The One Who is helping us
to hold fast today is the One
Who has called us.
I remain in deep wonder
at this.

Paul Favre-Miville, gardener, 46:
The grain
of the Good News
is germinating
deep
in the soil
of human hearts.
Let us be willing

that the Spirit
work
in us
through prayer
and a loving presence
for all.

Christophe Lebreton, carpenter, 46:
I feel called
to simply listen.
And it is God
Who is heard,
God Who is sent,
God Who tells me
to listen
and to welcome
all realities,
including my own.
May the Spirit
lead us
toward the full truth.

Christian de Cherge, priest, 59:
If it should happen one day—
and it could be today—
that I become a victim
of the terrorism
which engulfs
every foreigner in Algeria,
I would like my community
and my family

to remember
that my life
was given
to God
and to this country.
I ask them
to remember
that the Master of life
was no stranger
to a brutal departure.
I ask them
to pray for me,
that I be found worthy
of such an offering.
My life has no more value
than any other,
nor any less.
I have not the innocence
of childhood:
I have lived long enough
to know
that I am an accomplice
to the evil
which prevails
in the world.

I should like,
when the time comes,
to have a moment
of clarity
which would allow me

to beg forgiveness
of God
and of my fellow human beings,
and at the same time
forgive with all my heart
the one
who strikes me down.
My death will confirm
those who judge me naïve—
Let him tell us now of his ideals!—
but these persons should know
that my fiercest curiosity
will finally be set free,
for I shall be able
to immerse my gaze
in the gaze of the Father
and to contemplate with Him
all of His children,
just as He sees them—
each glistening
with glory
and abounding
with the Gifts of the Spirit,
whose secret joy is always
to establish communion
and cleanse our likenesses,
while delighting in our differences.

For this life lost,
totally mine and totally others,
I thank God,

Who has willed it entirely.
In this Thank You,
which is said for everything
in my life,
I include you,
my friends of yesterday and today,
and you, my friends of this place,
along with my mother and father,
my sisters and brothers and their families.
You are the hundredfold granted,
as was promised!

And you,
friend of my final moment,
who will not have known
what you were doing,
I thank you, too:
may this goodbye
be a blessing for you;
for deep within your face,
I see God's face.
May we meet again
as happy thieves in Paradise,
if it please God,
the Source of us both.
Amen!
Inchallah!

murdered by the world's joy

There is a spirit which is love unfeigned.
It never rejoiceth but through sufferings;
with the world's joy it is murdered.
—James Nayler

This is not a poem
about the goodness of love,
a poem pleading
for the return of love,
a poem that preaches
of love conquering fear.
I'm older, wearier
(winter is colder,
springtime briefer);
I no longer believe
in those kinds of love
(nor in those kinds of poems):
clergy sterilizing
our natural credo of joy
with say-so and doctrine;
politicians censuring abortion
with the same sirenic tongues
that lure the young
onto the rocks of war;
psychologists dousing
the pentecosts
of the human heart,
unaware that they fire

the Purpose
already there.

The Primal Bliss
roams (perfectly at peace)
beneath the tidy codes
of custom, law, protocol,
and the love that proceeds from it
bears suffering
without demanding justice,
withers all that is useless,
is naked in its hope.
This love (tethering us to freedom)
is lotus and thorn,
creation and cremation;
it experiments, fails;
behaves unseemly,
howling as it devours
the demons of pretense;
rejoices when we are crucified
in the dark mirror
of the world
and (finally) look
into that transparent face.

tell me my life again

Solitude, my mother, tell me my life again.
—Oskar Wladyslaw Milosz

I walk beneath boughs
round as water,
round as monk-mouths
crooning the *dies irae*
or *laudamus te.*
I walk slowly,
so the wind
will recognize me;
slowly,
so the snow can soak
my prayer-scorched skin,
and the sun's light, wan
but warm as Ephesian dust,
can remind me
of the True Psalm
I was born to profess,
the True Question
I was born to answer,
the True Desire
I was born to render.

I enter a grove
whose gate is a sword,
whose paths are strewn
with ginger grass.

I hear Hope.
She says—
I am here,
deep asleep
in swaddling clothes,
lying in the manger of your grief,
awaiting the Kiss
that will waken us both
from our dreams
of rape and apocalypse.
Smells waft and whisper,
Borrow us,
and in that instant,
my hands are salved,
my hair is scented,
and my clothes are perfumed
with myrrh.

A stranger's hand appears,
cupping a nectar.
He lifts it
to my lips,
and I drink
to the bottom
of his calloused palm
and lick the length
of each moist finger
to its tip—
and suddenly, I know:
this is the Garden
I wandered from.

Hope says—
Yes:
this is the Moment
within each moment,
when soul breathes you
into her silence,
separating reputation
from essence,
pain
from suffering,
greed
from longing;
joining your eye
with what it beholds,
your imagination
with wisdom,
your existence
with the Primal Mystery.
And then,
you are breathed out,
surrendered—
Word, once again,
inwoven with flesh.

only in silence

As we continue to unfurl our presence on earth,
must everything have a name and a use?
—Robert Perkins

Only in silence
do the tongueless speak—
tears,
rooms,
windows,
the wind.

Only in true
(not human)
silence
do the rocks cry out
and bread whispers
Break me.

Only the silence
(that requires
no witness)
can hear songs
hidden in dust
and bear the laughter
of the wakening land.

skin book, 7/2/03

We closed the longest chapter of our lives
when she died in our arms: Mother.
Shadows falling, falling
through the small window
of her basement bedroom.

—*Is she gone?* I ask.
—*She's been gone*
my brother says.
—*When?*
—*A couple of minutes ago—at 7:11.*

I look down at her again.
Her head looks different,
limper; her small hands,
smaller; her closed eyelids,
softer
(she is no longer trying to see).

—*Sing something*
someone says to me.
—*I can't think of anything to sing*
I say and lean back
against the closet door.

Then the kissing begins.

Anywhere—on her face,
on the top of her head,
up and down her arms.

—Oh, Helen!
Aunt Patsy Ruth wails,
in a voice of regret and confusion
that swathes my mother
in utter love and knowing.

By twos and ones,
they take slow leave—
sister, brother,
niece, nephews,
grandchildren and great-.
I,
her firstborn,
am here,
at last
alone with her.
I touch the skin
that held her life.
It is suddenly vast;
its grand silence
cannot be read.

She is here.
She is not here.
Her word
no longer
dwells among us.

She gave us
a good death,
and we helped her
with it.
Who am I now?

bread of the presence

South American Indians grind up the ashes and bones of dead parents and mix them in a soup which their children share, eating these new ancestors to gain their strength and virtues.
—Robin Fox

Real grief begins
when tears
are replaced
by chores;
when the lost face
and the stilled voice
are more forcibly fetched;
when certain objects—
an ashtray,
a spatula—
have returned
to their routine use;
when the hollows
of the heart
are no longer terrified
by the oil
of remembrance
and memories are,
at last,
allies.

Real grief begins
at the hearth

of sorrow,
where the ashes
of All That Matters
remain,
fresh and warm
and ready
for eating.
The whole name,
(the true Word)
of the beloved,
is swallowed
in silence
and laid to rest
within the primal script
of our eyes.

Real grief begins
when each breath
becomes an innocent gift
and the beloved's absence
tenderly echoes,
I Am Who Am.

mary's house: nightingale mountain

The nest of the nightingale
is neatly-lined with fibrous roots,
but the whole is so loosely constructed
that a very slight touch disturbs its beautiful arrangement.
—A.W. Mumford

Something pulls at me
from this small place,
a pull quite different
than what I am used to—
nothing noxious
or urgent.
I wonder:
is it the stones?
the plane trees'
quiet canopy?
the stillness deepening
with every step?

I cross the Gate
of the All Holy.
Two young nuns
on either side
of the open door
are recollecting God
in antiphonal chants
of sadness and joy.
All before me—

carpet, meek light,
lamp-blackened walls—
is as modest
as their voices—
straight-toned, mellow,
and impersonal.
Suddenly,
shoes, clothes,
even my face,
are no longer necessary;
neither are notions
of love
or life
or death.
I am saturate
with yearning.

I turn right
into an alcove.
In 1822,
a German mystic
saw Mary's death
in this room:
When she was dying
on her narrow couch,
she was lifted up
several times a day
and given juice
pressed from yellow berries.
Newcomers embraced
those already there.

After their feet
had been washed,
they approached Mary
and greeted her.
She could only say
a few words
to them.
One evening,
at about the ninth hour,
she lay back
on her round pillow
and died.
The house was closed.
Two women
washed the body
by lamplight.
John held a vessel
of spikenard.
Peter dipped a finger
into it
and anointed her breasts
and her hands and feet.
Myrrh was laid
in her armpits
and in the spaces between
her shoulders and neck
and her chin and cheeks.
A wreath
of red, white,
and sky-blue flowers
was placed on her bosom.

Her body was wrapped
in a great gravecloth
and placed
in a wicker coffin.

Today,
this is no longer
a room,
it is a moment
of perpetual *fiat*,
where everything
is held together—
not by molecules
or mercy
or art—
but by the wild alchemy
of innocence.
The only smell
of hell here
is the odor
of my ego
burning in the grease
of its own fear,
for in Mary's house,
there are no opposites:
peace replaces praise,
nativity is virginity,
the Virgin Heart
is announced
with each soft *hweet*
of the neighboring nightingales.

spooky action at a distance

*...subatomic particles are able to instantaneously
communicate with each other,
whether they are 10 feet or 10 billion miles apart.*
—Alain Aspect, physicist

*Billings Township Cemetery is well-kept, not very large,
and bordered on the west by the Tittabawassee River.
A sign tells you, "No Fishing From the Cemetery."*
—Victoria Warren, tombstone scribe

I have kin here
lying side-by-each,
their feet facing the river
that fed their lives
with motion and joy,
purpose and urgency—

Uncle Alfred,
who smoked black cigarettes,
and bought black Cadillacs,
and beat up Ann,
his common-law wife,
when he thought
she was giving particular eye
to any man
on the nights she sang
with the band
at Potter's Tavern;

Aunt Get and Uncle Jim,
who owned Get & Jim's Eat
and a bait shop
at the foot
of the Estey Road bridge.
Uncle Jim painted
FRENCH FRYS & CHILIE
in red enamel paint each spring
on the side of the restaurant
that faced the township hall.

Most mornings of the week,
'Pa-Leon, my grandfather,
sat himself just inside
the bait shop door
with a fifth of Schweppes,
a bag of gingersnaps,
and his blond cocker, Sandy,
and took coins
for the worms and minnies
that neighbors and tourists bought
for fishing off the bridge
or for ice fishing.

When I walk among
the ones now gone,
I pretend I can hear them.
Their voices are all-at-once
and faint at first,
stripes of sound—
a buzz, a hum, a whisper song—

soft as the onshore breeze
soughing at my ears.
Slowly though,
their fervor dims,
and then I hear,
clear as the tang
of pine pitch,
the single, lipless voice
in which they speak:
it is like good milk,
it is like a pair
of harboring hands,
it is like the large dog's
ruby-brown eyes.

It tells me:
We want you to know
that you are larger
than music,
more poetry
than circumstance,
have more than one future,
do not require
a savior.
Praise the security of chance,
the irrelevance of mortality,
the luxuries of oblivion.
Your task is to take
a long, black time
to escape the prisons
of family and personality.

Using the four elements—
desire, despair, biology, and wit—
remember and re-invent yourself
during your flesh-born days.
Live what you know
without offering
advice, answers,
or easy aphorisms,
and let what you don't know
enchant and sustain you.
Your imagination
is the seed and the history
of your hope:
the world
is wherever you are.
It is finished.
It is not finished.
It is finished.
It is never finished.
It is finished.
It is always beginning!

The words arrive
from an invisible
wing's width away:
they are old flowers
yearning to root
in the shadow I cast,
they are food
and mantle
for the silver trail;
they turn my feet
toward the river.

why do poems come

Why do poems come
in the middle
of the night—
like dreams
or hunger pangs
or a memory
suddenly snapping
to attention
for minute inspection?

Once arrived,
they quickly become
demanding—
like destiny
or a lover's tongue
or a babe biting
the nipple
for *more* milk,
more *milk*,
more milk;

demanding a place
outside the night
where their teethmarks
can be seen
and their edges
scraped

and their backs
patted
and soothed.

Poems are ingrates,
that give
no thought
to the oughts
of time,
to the body's need
for rhythmic ease;
are unsleeping
like love,
that veil-render,
whose wild blessings
unite day and night
and prescribe
the ointment of paradise
to the vilest
of thieves.

about the author

Rusty C. Moe is the author of two previous works of poetry, *Our Presence Together In Chaos* and *Where God Learns*, both published by Black Moss Press. A native of Midland, Michigan, he is a graduate of Saginaw Valley College (English and psychology), United Theological Seminary (counseling and religious studies), Butler University (creative writing) and holds certificates from the School of Spiritual Psychology and the Gestalt Institutes of Indianapolis and Cleveland. He is an instructor with the Indianapolis Gestalt Institute and the Creative Spirit Center. He is a supervisor in the marriage and family therapy program at Christian Theological Seminary. He has been, for many years, a psychotherapist in private practice in Indianapolis, Indiana, where he lives with his partner, Tim Hoover.

Printed in the United States
77993LV00007B/259-306